LEARNING HEBREW: THINGS THAT GO!

Activity Book for Beginners

Learning Hebrew: Things that go! Activity Book for Beginners

Bible Pathway Adventures® is a trademark of BPA Publishing Ltd.

ISBN: 978-1-98-858549-9

Authors: Pip Reid
Creative Director: Curtis Reid

For free Bible resources including coloring pages, worksheets, puzzles and more, visit our website at:

www.biblepathwayadventures.com

www.biblepathwayadventures.com
Learning Hebrew: Things that go! Activity Book

2

© BPA Publishing Ltd 2020

Introduction for Parents

Have fun teaching your children the Hebrew names for transportation with our *Learning Hebrew Activity Book: Things that go!* From boat to bicycle to truck to tractor, there are 22 Hebrew words to teach them. Plus, plenty of opportunities for them to practice coloring and writing what they've learned.

This book is designed to build on the foundation laid in our Learning Hebrew: The Alphabet Activity Book. We created both books to help you teach your children the basics of the Hebrew language in a fun and creative way. Children exposed to Hebrew, especially those growing in their knowledge of Torah, will gain increased Biblical understanding and a deeper love for Yah's Word.

Bible Pathway Adventures helps educators and parents teach children a Biblical Faith in a fun creative way. We do this via our illustrated storybooks, teacher packs, and printable activities – available for download on our website www.biblepathwayadventures.com

The search for Truth is more fun than Tradition!

 Table of Contents

www.biblepathwayadventures.com
Learning Hebrew: Things that go! Activity Book

4

© BPA Publishing Ltd 2020

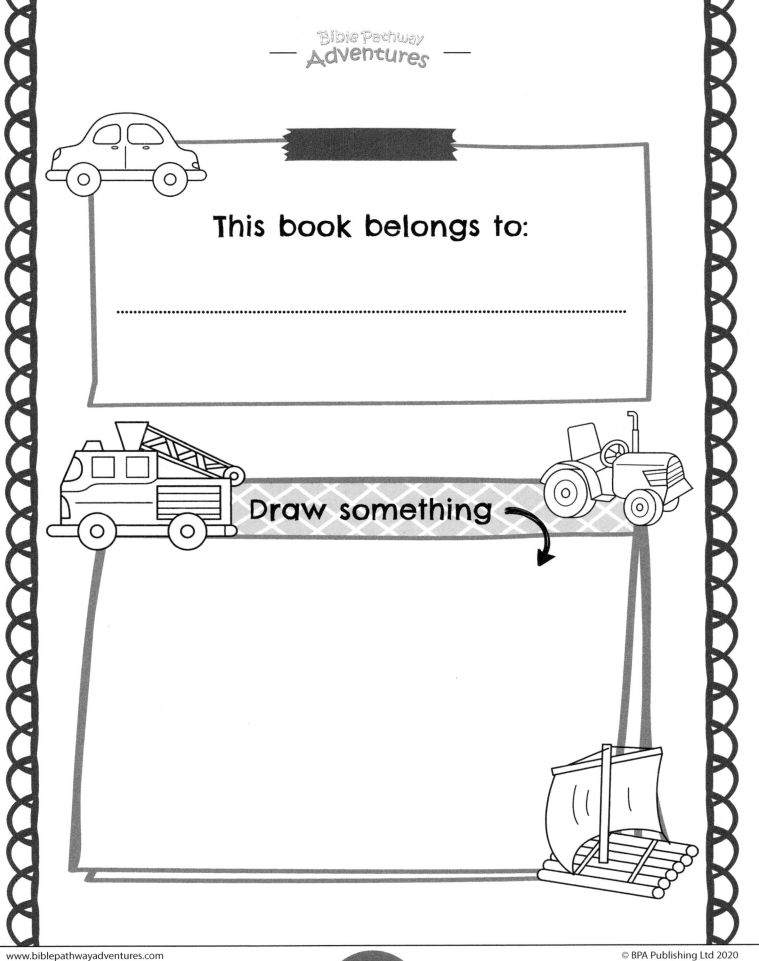

This book belongs to:

....

Draw something

www.biblepathwayadventures.com
Learning Hebrew: Things that go! Activity Book

5

© BPA Publishing Ltd 2020

The Hebrew Alphabet

	Modern	Paleo	Pictograph
Aleph			
Bet			
Gimmel			
Dalet			
Hey			
Vav			
Zayin			
Het			
Tet			
Yod			
Kaph			
Lamed			
Mem			
Nun			
Samech			
Ayin			
Peh			
Tsadi			
Qoph			
Resh			
Shin			
Tav			

 # Did you know?

Hebrew is written and read from right to left.

Hebrew is one of the original languages of the Bible.

There are twenty-two letters in the Hebrew alphabet.

The Hebrew alphabet has no vowels.

When you learn Hebrew, vowels are added to words in the form of small dots. These appear above, below, or inside a letter. This system of dots and dashes (called nikkudot or nikkud) shows you how to pronounce a Hebrew word.

הִיפּוֹפּוֹטָם

www.biblepathwayadventures.com
Learning Hebrew: Things that go! Activity Book

7

© BPA Publishing Ltd 2020

★ Mechonit ★

The Hebrew word for car is mechonit. A car is a road vehicle used to carry people. Rich Israelites were carried from place to place in horse-drawn chariots.

mechonit

מְכוֹנִית

car

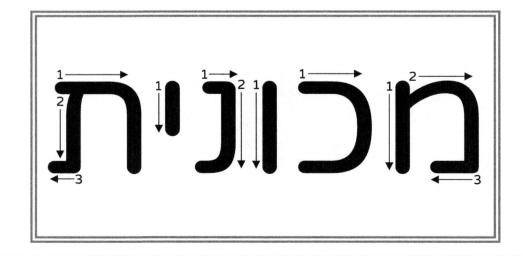

Let's write!

Practice writing this Hebrew word on the lines below.

Try this on your own.
Remember that Hebrew is read from RIGHT to LEFT.

✹ Monit ✹

The Hebrew word for taxi is monit. A taxi is used to take people and things from place to place. The Israelites used carts instead of taxis to do the same thing.

monit

מוֹנִית

taxi

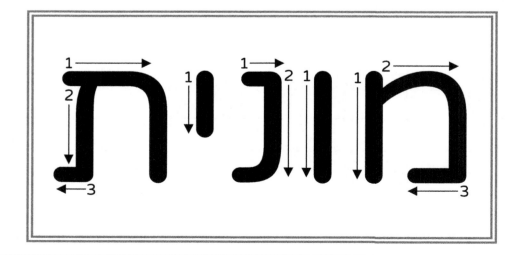

www.biblepathwayadventures.com
Learning Hebrew: Things that go! Activity Book

10

© BPA Publishing Ltd 2020

Let's write!

Practice writing this Hebrew word on the lines below.

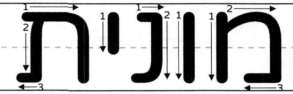

Try this on your own.
Remember that Hebrew is read from RIGHT to LEFT.

www.biblepathwayadventures.com
Learning Hebrew: Things that go! Activity Book

11

✶ Rakkevet ✶

The Hebrew word for train is rakkevet. A train is a set of wagons (or cars) on a railway. Joseph sent wagons back to the land of Canaan to transport his family to Egypt.

rakkevet

רַכֶּבֶת

train

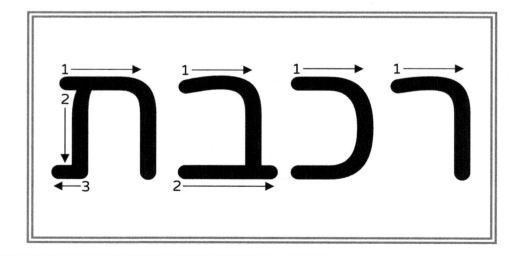

www.biblepathwayadventures.com
Learning Hebrew: Things that go! Activity Book

12

© BPA Publishing Ltd 2020

Let's write!

Practice writing this Hebrew word on the lines below.

Try this on your own.
Remember that Hebrew is read from RIGHT to LEFT.

www.biblepathwayadventures.com
Learning Hebrew: Things that go! Activity Book

13

✦ Otobbus ✦

The Hebrew word for bus is otobbus. A bus is a large vehicle used for carrying people. The ancient Israelites did not have buses; they usually walked everywhere.

otobbus

אוֹטוֹבּוּס

bus

Let's write!

Practice writing this Hebrew word on the lines below.

אוטובוס

אוטובוס

Try this on your own.
Remember that Hebrew is read from RIGHT to LEFT.

www.biblepathwayadventures.com
Learning Hebrew: Things that go! Activity Book

15

✦ Matos ✦

The Hebrew word for plane is matos. A plane is a machine that can fly. The Israelites used boats, camels, and horses to travel long distances.

matos

מָטוֹס

plane

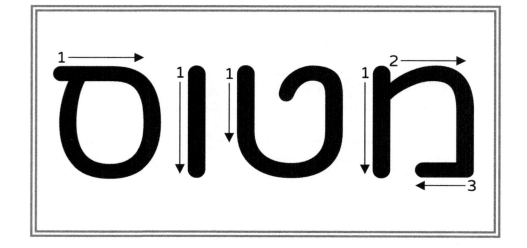

Let's write!

Practice writing this Hebrew word on the lines below.

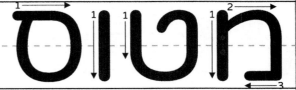

Try this on your own.
Remember that Hebrew is read from RIGHT to LEFT.

Learning Hebrew: Things that go! Activity Book

✸ Masok ✸

The Hebrew word for helicopter is masok. A helicopter lifts up off the ground like a bee. During disasters, helicopters take food to people who cannot be reached by road.

masok

מַסוֹק

helicopter

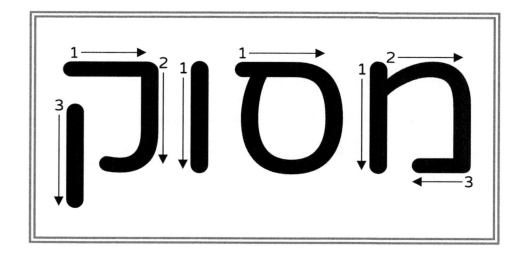

Let's write!

Practice writing this Hebrew word on the lines below.

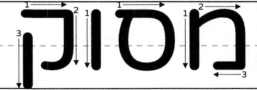

מסוכ

Try this on your own.
Remember that Hebrew is read from RIGHT to LEFT.

⭐ Chalalit ⭐

The Hebrew word for rocket is chalalit.
A rocket is usually shaped like an arrow.
Rockets work using fire and can fly very fast.

chalalit

חֲלָלִית

rocket

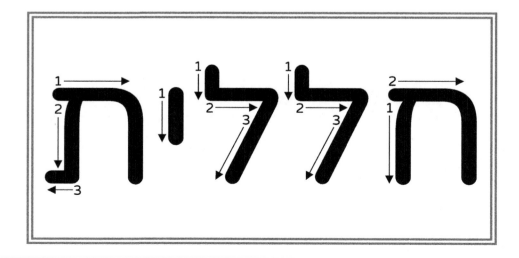

www.biblepathwayadventures.com
Learning Hebrew: Things that go! Activity Book

20

© BPA Publishing Ltd 2020

Let's write!

Practice writing this Hebrew word on the lines below.

חללית

Try this on your own.
Remember that Hebrew is read from RIGHT to LEFT.

www.biblepathwayadventures.com
Learning Hebrew: Things that go! Activity Book

21

✸ Kabba'it ✸

The Hebrew word for fire truck is kabba'it.
The ancient Israelites didn't have fire trucks like we do today.
They used hand-operated pumps to put out fires.

kabba'it

כַּבָּאִית

fire truck

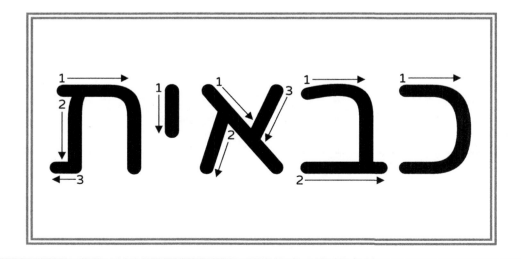

Let's write!

Practice writing this Hebrew word on the lines below.

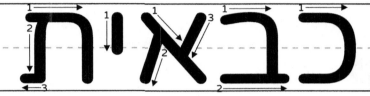

Try this on your own.
Remember that Hebrew is read from RIGHT to LEFT.

✦ Teraktor ✦

The Hebrew word for tractor is teraktor. Tractors are used on farms to pull tools and trailers. The Israelites did not have tractors; instead they used oxen to pull plows.

teraktor

טְרַקְטוֹר

tractor

Let's write!

Practice writing this Hebrew word on the lines below.

טרקטור

Try this on your own.
Remember that Hebrew is read from RIGHT to LEFT.

www.biblepathwayadventures.com
Learning Hebrew: Things that go! Activity Book

25

✦ Ofanoa ✦

The Hebrew word for motorbike is ofanoa. A motorbike has two wheels and can carry another person. The Israelites used two-wheeled carts pulled by donkeys.

ofanoa

אוֹפַנוֹעַ

motorbike

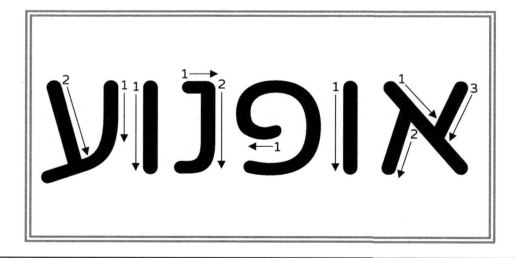

Let's write!

Practice writing this Hebrew word on the lines below.

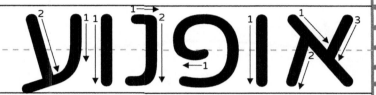

אופנוע

Try this on your own.
Remember that Hebrew is read from RIGHT to LEFT.

✸ Katnoa ✸

The Hebrew word for scooter is katnoa. Scooters have a basket or space below the seat to carry goods. The Israelites used donkeys to take goods from place to place.

katnoa

קַטְנוֹעַ

scooter

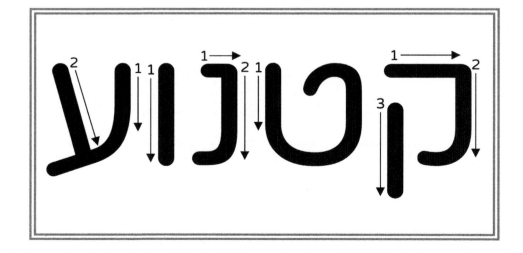

Let's write!

Practice writing this Hebrew word on the lines below.

קטנוע

Try this on your own.
Remember that Hebrew is read from RIGHT to LEFT.

✶ Ofanayim ✶

The Hebrew word for bicycle is ofanayim. A bicycle has two wheels, two pedals, and a metal chain. The Israelites used animals to help them get from place to place.

ofanayim

אוֹפַנַּיִם

bicycle

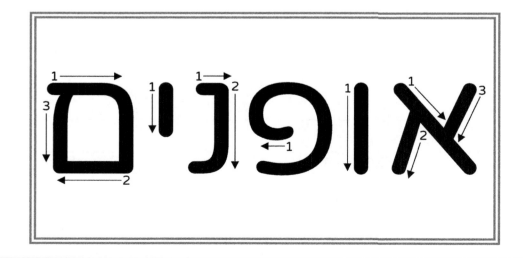

Let's write!

Practice writing this Hebrew word on the lines below.

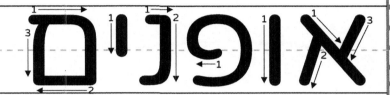

אופנים

אופנים

Try this on your own.
Remember that Hebrew is read from RIGHT to LEFT.

www.biblepathwayadventures.com
Learning Hebrew: Things that go! Activity Book

31

✶ Masa'it ✶

The Hebrew word for truck is masa'it. Trucks are used to take goods from one place to another. The Israelites used carts to transport goods like grain and storage jars.

masa'it

מַשָּׂאִית

truck

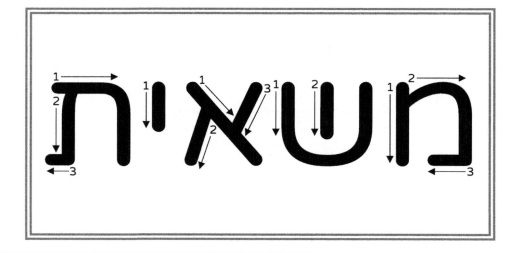

Let's write!

Practice writing this Hebrew word on the lines below.

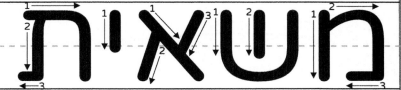

מַשָׂאִית

Try this on your own.
Remember that Hebrew is read from RIGHT to LEFT.

⭐ Rikeshah ⭐

The Hebrew word for rickshaw is rikeshah. A rickshaw is a small vehicle used in countries like India. Rich Israelites used horse-drawn chariots to get from place to place.

rikeshah

רִיקְקְשָׁה

rickshaw

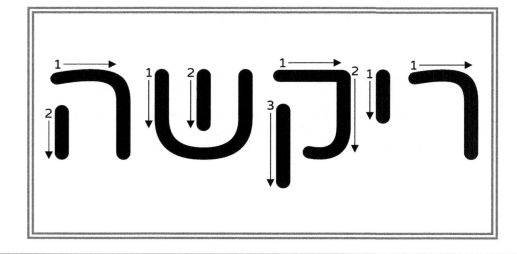

Let's write!

Practice writing this Hebrew word on the lines below.

Try this on your own.
Remember that Hebrew is read from RIGHT to LEFT.

✵ Tzolelet ✵

The Hebrew word for submarine is tzolelet. A submarine is a vessel that moves under water. People use submarines to find shipwrecks and living things under the sea.

Tzolelet

צוֹלֶלֶת

submarine

www.biblepathwayadventures.com
Learning Hebrew: Things that go! Activity Book

36

© BPA Publishing Ltd 2020

Let's write!

Practice writing this Hebrew word on the lines below.

צוללת

Try this on your own.
Remember that Hebrew is read from RIGHT to LEFT.

www.biblepathwayadventures.com
Learning Hebrew: Things that go! Activity Book

37

✶ Sirah ✶

The Hebrew word for boat is sirah.
The Israelites made boats out of cedar wood and nails.
They used boats for transportation and fishing.

sirah

סִירָה

boat

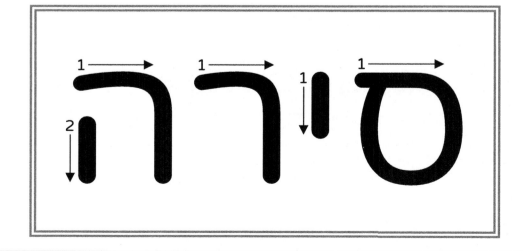

Let's write!

Practice writing this Hebrew word on the lines below.

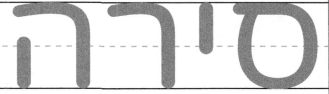

Try this on your own.
Remember that Hebrew is read from RIGHT to LEFT.

✬ Kayak ✬

The Hebrew word for kayak is kayak. A kayak is a small boat used for fishing, exploring, and hunting. The ancient Egyptians made kayaks from reeds (papyrus).

kayak

קַיָאק

kayak

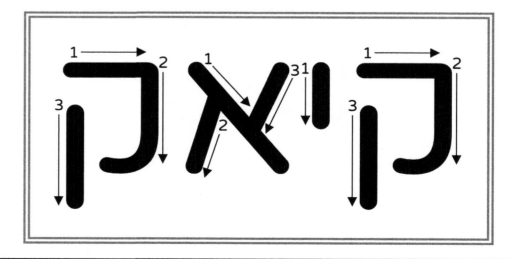

www.biblepathwayadventures.com
Learning Hebrew: Things that go! Activity Book

40

© BPA Publishing Ltd 2020

Let's write!

Practice writing this Hebrew word on the lines below.

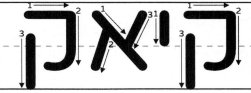

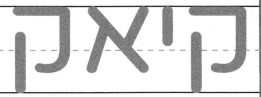

Try this on your own.
Remember that Hebrew is read from RIGHT to LEFT.

www.biblepathwayadventures.com
Learning Hebrew: Things that go! Activity Book

41

© BPA Publishing Ltd 2020

✦ Sefinah ✦

The Hebrew word for ship is sefinah. The Phoenicians built King Solomon a fleet of ships. They sailed all over the world and found gold, silver, and peacocks.

sefinah

סְפִינָה

ship

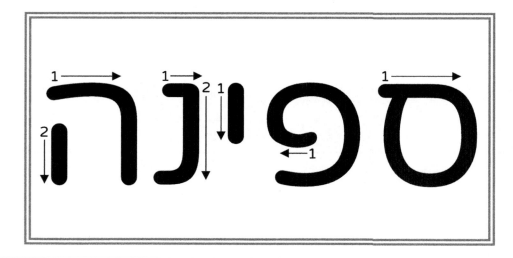

www.biblepathwayadventures.com
Learning Hebrew: Things that go! Activity Book

42

© BPA Publishing Ltd 2020

Let's write!

Practice writing this Hebrew word on the lines below.

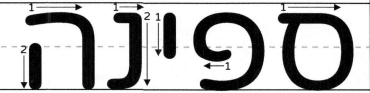

ספינה

Try this on your own.
Remember that Hebrew is read from RIGHT to LEFT.

✸ Rafsodah ✸

The Hebrew word for raft is rafsodah. The king of Lebanon made trees into rafts. He floated them on the sea to the land of Israel so Solomon could build a temple.

rafsodah

רַפְסֹדָה

raft

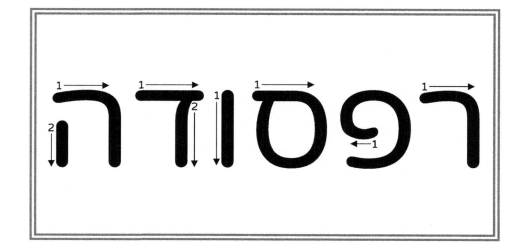

www.biblepathwayadventures.com
Learning Hebrew: Things that go! Activity Book

44

© BPA Publishing Ltd 2020

Let's write!

Practice writing this Hebrew word on the lines below.

רפסודה

רפסודה

Try this on your own.
Remember that Hebrew is read from RIGHT to LEFT.

✶ Sus ✶

The Hebrew word for horse is sus. Horses can sleep lying down or standing up. During the Exodus, the Egyptians chased after the Israelites with horses and chariots.

sus

סוּס

horse

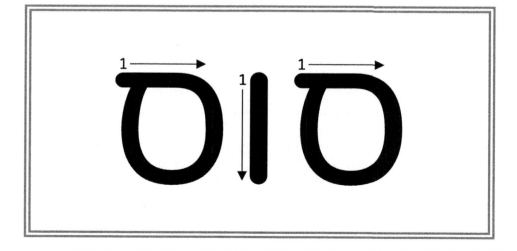

Let's write!

Practice writing this Hebrew word on the lines below.

סוס

סוס

Try this on your own.
Remember that Hebrew is read from RIGHT to LEFT.

www.biblepathwayadventures.com
Learning Hebrew: Things that go! Activity Book

47

✦ Gamal ✦

The Hebrew word for camel is gamal.
When Abraham's servant went to Mesopotamia to find
a wife for Isaac, he took ten camels with him.

gamal

גָּמָל

camel

Let's write!

Practice writing this Hebrew word on the lines below.

גמל

Try this on your own.
Remember that Hebrew is read from RIGHT to LEFT.

www.biblepathwayadventures.com
Learning Hebrew: Things that go! Activity Book

49

✦ Chamor ✦

The Hebrew word for donkey is chamor. The Israelites used donkeys to transport goods and pull plows. Jacob's sons brought grain back from Egypt on donkeys (Gen 42).

chamor

חֲמוֹר

donkey

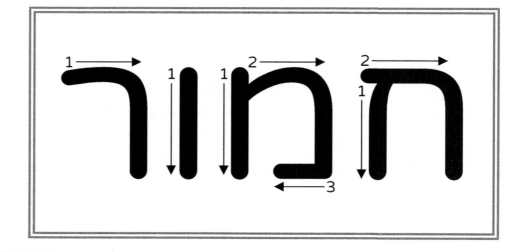

Let's write!

Practice writing this Hebrew word on the lines below.

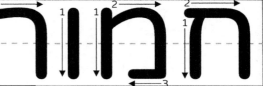

Try this on your own.
Remember that Hebrew is read from RIGHT to LEFT.

🌿 Trace the Words 🌿

Trace the words. Color the pictures.

❧ Trace the Words ❧

Trace the words. Color the pictures.

🌿 Trace the Words 🌿

Trace the words. Color the pictures.

www.biblepathwayadventures.com
Learning Hebrew: Things that go! Activity Book

54

© BPA Publishing Ltd 2020

🌿 Trace the Words 🌿

Trace the words. Color the pictures.

🌿 Trace the Words 🌿

Trace the words. Color the pictures.

	קַיִן
	סְפִינָה
	רַפְסוֹדָה
	סוּס

❧ Trace the Words ❧

Trace the words. Color the pictures.

FLASHCARDS

🌿 Flashcards 🌿

Color and cut out the flashcards.
Hang them around your home or classroom!

Mechonit / Car

1

Monit / Taxi

2

Rakkevet / Train

3

Otobbus / Bus

4

www.biblepathwayadventures.com
Learning Hebrew: Things that go! Activity Book

59

✂

מטוס

Matos / Plane

5

מסוק

Masok / Helicopter

6

חללית

Chalalit / Rocket

7

כבאית

Kabba'it / Fire truck

8

www.biblepathwayadventures.com
Learning Hebrew: Things that go! Activity Book

61

© BPA Publishing Ltd 2020

טרקטור

Teraktor / Tractor

9

אופנוע

Ofanoa / Motorbike

10

קטנוע

Katnoa / Scooter

11

אופנים

Ofanayim / Bicycle

12

משאית

Masa'it / Truck

13

ריקשה

RikeShah / RickShaw

14

צוללת

Tzolelet / Submarine

15

סירה

Sirah / Boat

16

www.biblepathwayadventures.com
Learning Hebrew: Things that go! Activity Book

65

✂

קיאק

Kayak / Kayak

17

ספינה

Sefinah / Ship

18

רפסודה

Rafsodah / Raft

19

סוס

Sus / Horse

20

גמל

Gamal / Camel

25

חמור

Chamor / Donkey

26

www.biblepathwayadventures.com
Learning Hebrew: Things that go! Activity Book

69

© BPA Publishing Ltd 2020

Discover more Activity Books!

Available for purchase at www.biblepathwayadventures.com

INSTANT DOWNLOAD!

Learning Hebrew: The Alphabet
Learning Hebrew: Animals
Learning Hebrew: Around the home
Learning Hebrew: Let's Eat!
Learning Hebrew: Things that go!
Learning Hebrew: Fruit & Vegetables
Learning Hebrew: Clothes
Clean & Unclean

www.biblepathwayadventures.com
Learning Hebrew: Things that go! Activity Book

70

© BPA Publishing Ltd 2020